//*As Big as They Come*//

BY

JANICE

LEITCH

Illustrations by
Kylie Baker

Last year our Uncle Barney grew the biggest carrot in the world. You won't find it listed in the Guiness Book of Records and no one even took a photo of it for the paper, but it was big all right.

It all started in the spring when we noticed Uncle Barney digging a huge hole in the vegetable garden. We watched (and held our noses) while he lowered a very dead sheep into the hole. He covered it up, put in several shovelfuls of fertiliser, then one carrot seed.

"Just one seed?" asked Aunty Kay. "Surely a hole like that could take a whole packet of seeds."

"I know what I'm doing," said Uncle Barney.

All through the rest of the spring and the summer Uncle Barney watered that carrot seed. Sometimes he gave it coffee, sometimes tea. It wasn't long before the carrot poked through the ground. Uncle Barney gave it more fertiliser and more tea. The carrot grew and grew until soon the leaves were as big as several ferns in the bush.

One day, in late summer, Uncle Barney said, "I think it's time we dug that carrot up."
"Do you need any help?" my sister Melanie asked.
"Stick around, I just might."
We watched while Uncle Barney dug a huge ring around the carrot.
"It can't be that big," gasped Melanie.
"I think it might be," said Uncle Barney. He grasped the leaves and started to pull. He went red in the face as he yanked and tugged at the carrot.
"Think I need you two and Aunty Kay," he huffed at last.
Aunty Kay had been watching and she came over. She grasped Uncle Barney around the waist. Melanie held on to her and I grabbed hold of Melanie. We pulled and pulled, but still the carrot wouldn't budge.

"Looks like I'll have to get the tractor," said Uncle Barney. When he finally got the old tractor started he tied a rope from it to the carrot top. He slowly backed the tractor away and Snap! The rope broke. Next Uncle Barney tied two stronger ropes around the carrot. Then he backed the tractor once more. This time we heard a plop and the carrot slid out of the ground.
"What are you going to do now?" we asked Uncle Barney.
"Think I'll put it in the show," he replied. "Sure to get a prize for the biggest carrot."

The next weekend we all helped Uncle Barney to load the giant carrot on to the back of his truck. We were huffing and puffing by the time we got it tied down.
"You coming to the show?" asked Uncle Barney when we had finished.
"You bet!" We wanted to hear what everyone would say when they saw the giant carrot. We piled into the truck, buckled up and were off.
"Think I'll take the coast road," said Uncle Barney. "Don't want to cause any accidents by people staring at our carrot and not looking at the road."

It was fun going on the coast road. When we passed horses and donkeys we yelled at them, "Bet you wish you could have our carrot."
A farmer driving a flock of sheep along the road asked us if we were going to make carrot soup for the whole army.
"Might just do that," laughed Uncle Barney.
But then, at the next corner, a dreadful thing happened.

Right at the highest point of the road with the sea far below us we heard a loud twang. The ropes holding the carrot had frayed and snapped. Uncle Barney chose that moment to hit the biggest pothole on the road. Thumpity bump, the carrot bounced off the truck.

The last sight we had of the biggest carrot in the world was when it bounced down the hillside and into the sea. We were all very quiet. I expected Uncle Barney to be angry. But he just shrugged and turned the truck around.

"These things happen," he said. "I'll grow another carrot next year. It'll be even bigger than that one. I'll get some stronger rope and we'll take the inland road to the show."